DATE DUE

DEC 27 2005		
FEB 28 2006		
AUG 19 2008		
SEP 21 2010		
JAN 19 2011		
DEC 21 2011		
OCT 15 2012		
FEB 11 2013		

#47-0108 Peel Off Pressure Sensitive

Animal Lives

BEARS

Sally Morgan

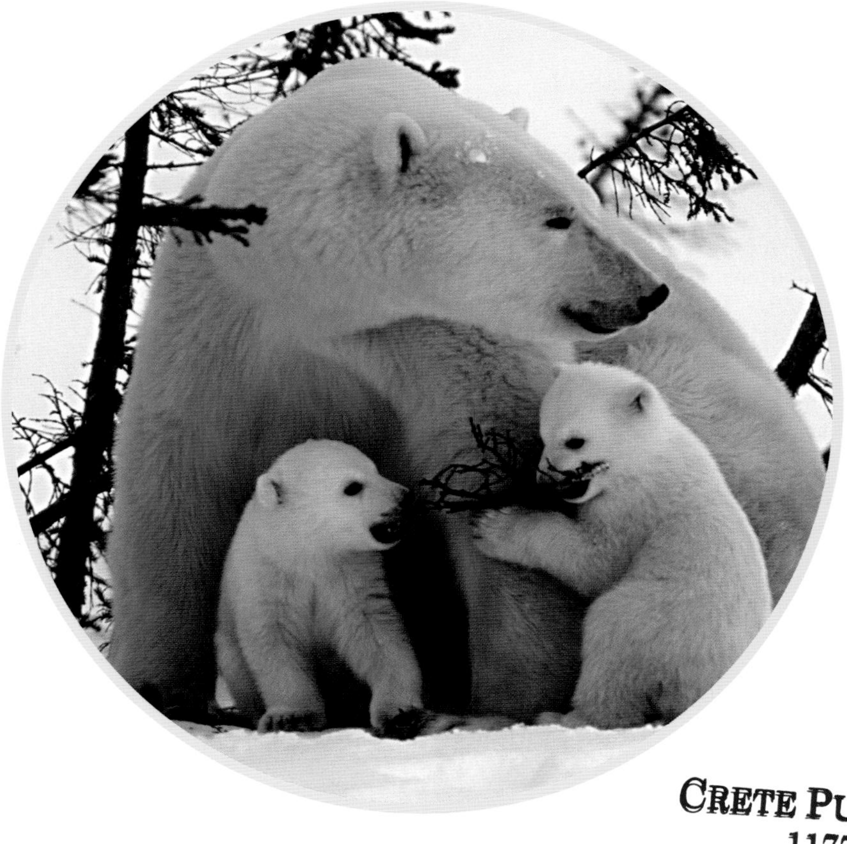

QEB Publishing

Library of Congress Control Number
2004101320

ISBN 1-59566-033-X

Written by Sally Morgan
Designed by Tall Tree Books
Editor Christine Harvey
Map by PCGraphics (UK) Ltd

Creative Director Louise Morley
Editorial Manager Jean Coppendale

Printed and bound in China

The words in **bold** are
explained in the Glossary
on page 31.

Contents

The bear

Bears are some of the best-known animals in the world. Bears have a heavy body and thick legs. Their head is large, and they have a big nose and small eyes. They have large feet called paws. Each of their toes ends in a long, sharp claw.

The brown bear has very thick, dark brown fur. It has a wide neck and powerful shoulders.

The sun bear gets its name from the markings on the front of its body

Bear

Bears often stand up on their back legs. They do this to get a better view, or a better smell, of what is ahead of them. Sometimes they stand up to threaten another bear.

fact

Mammals

Bears belong to a group of animals called mammals. Like most mammals, female bears give birth to live young and produce milk for them.

Bears are covered with fur. This helps them stay warm. Their body temperature hardly changes, even when the temperature around them does.

Bear types

There are eight species, or types, of bear. The brown bear is called the grizzly because the hairs on its back and shoulders are sometimes tipped in white, giving it a 'grizzled' appearance. Other species of bear are the American black bear, the Asian black bear, the sun bear, the sloth bear, and the spectacled bear.

Most bears have fur that is black, brown, or white. The polar bear is the only completely white bear.

Giant panda cubs stay with their mothers for up to three years.

6

Small bears

The Asian black bear, sun bear, sloth bear, and spectacled bear are much smaller than the other bears. The sun bear is the smallest.

A sloth bear has no front teeth, so it can suck up termites from their nests.

The American and Asian black bears look similar. However, the Asian black bear has a crescent-shaped white patch on its chest that gives it its other name—"moon bear."

American black bears can go without food for up to seven months during hibernation.

Bear

American black bears are not always black. They come in all shades of brown and a few are white!

fact

7

Where do you find bears?

Polar bears are found mainly in the Arctic, where it is cold all year round. Brown bears are found across North America, northern Europe, and Asia. They live in different **habitats**, including forests and open ground. Giant pandas are found only in central China, where they live in bamboo forests.

Bear

Polar bears spend as much time on the ice as they do on land. Small, soft bumps on the pads of their feet stop them from slipping.

fact

Polar bears are found in Alaska, Canada, Russia, Denmark and Norway.

North America	Europe	Asia
Atlantic Ocean	Africa	Pacific Ocean
Pacific Ocean	South America	Indian Ocean
		Australia
	Southern Ocean	
	Antarctica	

□ Areas where bears are found.

Other bears

Spectacled bears live in forests in South America. Sloth bears are found in different habitats in India. Sun bears live in forests in South-East Asia. Black bears live in forest areas in America and Asia.

The American black bear is found across North America and in Mexico

9

Living in the Arctic

Polar bears are well suited to living in the icy world of the Arctic. Polar bears have large bodies that are covered in thick, white fur. The only parts of their bodies not covered in fur are their black noses and the pads on the bottom of their feet.

The polar bear's white fur is good camouflage against the snow.

Keeping warm

Polar bears have black skin. Black is a good color in the Arctic, because it **absorbs** heat. Beneath their skin is a thick layer of fat called blubber. The fat helps keep the bear warm, because it stops heat escaping from their bodies.

A polar bear's feet are partly webbed.

A polar bear is so well **insulated** with fur and fat that it loses hardly any heat. In fact, it is not unusual for an adult bear to overheat when it runs.

Polar bears lie on the ice to cool down.

11

Beginning life

A female bear is ready to mate when she reaches four to five years of age. After mating, she is **pregnant** for seven to eight months.

A newborn bear cub is small. It is about the size of a guinea pig. Cubs are born blind and without fur. They **suckle** their mother's milk for six months before they start to eat solid food.

Bear

Most bear cubs weigh between 7–11 ounces. Polar bear cubs are slightly heavier at about 1–1½ pounds.

fact

A female bear gives birth to a litter of one to three cubs.

Bear cubs stay close to their mother for the first few months.

Dens

Bears that live in cold climates spend the winter in a **den**. Their cubs are born in the den in the middle of winter. The cubs stay with their mother in the den for three months. In early spring, the temperature gets warmer and the bear leads her cubs outside for the first time.

In the Arctic, the female polar bear digs out a hole under the snow where she gives birth to her cubs.

Growing up

When the cubs come out of the den their mother shows them what foods are good to eat. After six months, bear cubs grow their adult teeth.

The cubs spend a lot of time playing with each other. The mother growls or grunts at her cubs if they misbehave. If they do not listen to her warnings, she knocks them over with her paw.

Bear cubs follow their mother everywhere, learning from everything she does.

Living in territories

Bear cubs stay with their mother for up to four years. Then the young bears move away.

Adult bears live on their own in one area. This is their **territory**. The female bear raises her cubs on her own, without any help from the male bear. When the young bears leave their mother, they have to find a territory of their own.

Polar bear cubs like to "play-fight" They often stand up like boxers or roll on the ground like wrestlers.

15

Hunting

Polar bears and brown bears are **predators**. They have sharp teeth and long claws to grip their **prey**. The polar bear is a **carnivore**. It hunts by stalking or by lying in wait for its prey. Sometimes the polar bear will crawl over the ice toward its prey, charging when it is close. At other times, it sits beside a hole in the ice, waiting for a seal to come up to breathe. When the seal comes up, the bear bites it and drags it onto the ice. Polar bear cubs learn to hunt by watching their mother.

A seal provides enough food to feed
a polar bear for about eight days.

Fishing for food

Brown bears feed on a variety of food, such as fish, insects, and berries. They are **omnivores**. In the fall, they fish in rivers. The bears wade into the water and catch salmon as they swim past. The young cubs practice by standing in shallow water, trying to catch the salmon.

Brown bears grip the slippery salmon in their claws or teeth.

Eating

Brown bears and polar bears have four long teeth called canines at the front of their mouth. They use these teeth to grab their prey. They also have large teeth called molars that crush bones and slice through meat.

Smaller bears eat a mixed diet of insects, fruit, and honey. The sloth bear breaks open termite nests with its sharp claws and sucks up hundreds of termites. The sun bear spends much of the day in the trees searching for food. It sticks its tongue into holes to find termites and to lick up honey from bees' nests.

The sun bear uses its long tongue to find food.

The giant panda

Giant pandas are the odd bears out, as they are **herbivores**. They eat only plants, especially bamboo shoots. They are born with a special bone in their wrists that sticks out. They use this bone, together with their thumbs, to grip bamboo stems. Giant pandas have strong jaws and cheek muscles to crush the thick stalks.

Bear

As they get older, bears lose their teeth and eventually may starve to death because they can't chew their food.

fact

Giant pandas spend at least sixteen hours a day eating bamboo.

19

Bear senses

Like human babies, bear cubs are born with all their senses and have to learn to use them. Polar bears have the best eyesight and can see well underwater. Most bears are short-sighted. This means they can see things that are close to them very well—for example, food—but they are not very good at seeing things in the distance.

A bear's sense of smell is better than its sight.

Smell

A bear's sense of smell is better than a human's. Bears rely on their sense of smell to find food, identify their cubs, and find a mate. A good sense of smell allows them to detect and avoid danger, in the form of other bears and humans. A polar bear has a very good sense of smell and can detect its prey on the ice many miles away.

Bears leave their scent around the edge of their territory to let other bears know they should not enter.

Moving

Bears walk slowly with their heads swinging gently from side to side. Most bears walk a little like humans. They walk on the soles of their feet with their heels touching the ground first. Bears can also stand on their back feet and walk upright for short distances.

Although they walk slowly, some bears can run fast. An American black bear can run at 35 miles per hour for a short distance. That is about as fast as a horse or a deer.

Bears can run faster than humans. Once they start running, they find it difficult to stop quickly.

Bear
The Kodiak bear, a type of brown bear, weighs as much as half a ton, but can move quickly, at speeds of up to 30 miles per hour.

fact

Polar bears can swim for long distances and even dive under the ice.

Swimming and climbing

Polar bears are excellent swimmers. They swim by paddling with their huge front paws. They use their back legs to steer.

Many bears can climb, too. The sun bear has very long claws to grip the trunks of trees as it climbs. Sometimes it hugs the tree with its front legs and hauls itself up with its teeth!

American black bears climb into trees to find food, such as buds, fruit, and nuts.

23

Hibernation

Black and brown bears that live in colder parts of the world spend the winter in a deep sleep. This sleep is called hibernation. Bears hibernate because the weather is too cold for them and there is no food. Polar bears do not hibernate. They are active all year round.

A female American black bear and her cub have crawled under a large log to hibernate.

Getting ready to hibernate

In the fall, adult bears and cubs eat a lot of food to build up their body fat, ready for their hibernation. Then they look for a place to hibernate, such as a cave or a hollow under a fallen tree. Bears spend up to six months hibernating, without food or water. They live off their body fat. Female bears give birth to their cubs while hibernating. The cubs then hibernate with their mother the following winter.

Bear

It is not unusual for a bear to lose one-third of its body weight while it is hibernating.

fact

Spirit bears are white-colored black bears. They are very rare.

25

Bears and people

Bears can be dangerous animals. The female bear is especially dangerous when she has cubs. She defends her cubs from predators, such as wolves and mountain lions. She will also attack humans, if they come too close to her cubs.

Some bears have learned that where there are people, there is food. They raid campsites and cars looking for food. Some visit garbage dumps to find food.

Polar bears visit garbage dumps to find food.

Bears in towns

Some bears go into towns and suburbs looking for food. People living in these areas try to stop the bears. They make sure the bears can't find food or garbage. They use special trash cans that the bears can't get into.

Many bears are attracted to places in the countryside where people have dumped garbage.

Bear

Because bears can't see things in the distance very well, they may mistake a person for a predator or another bear, and attack them by mistake.

fact

Bears under threat

The number of bears around the world has fallen in the last 100 years. There were once 100,000 brown bears in North America; now there are only a few thousand. The rarest bear is the giant panda—there are only 1000 left.

Bears have been hunted by humans for sport but in some areas, such as northern Canada, tourists travel to watch bears in their natural habitat. Special trucks called polar rovers take them out on the ice to see the polar bears.

People are not allowed to get too close or to get out of the polar rover because polar bears are very dangerous.

Habitats

Bears have lost their **habitats** because forests have been cleared for lumber. Giant panda bears are under threat because there are very few bamboo forests left.

Polar bears are suffering because of climate change. This means that the ice breaks up much earlier each year, which stops the polar bears from hunting.

Today, many bears are protected. They live in national parks and nature reserves where they can't be hunted.

Spectacled bears have white markings around their nose and eyes. They live in forests in South America.

29

Life cycle

A female bear is pregnant for eight months. She gives birth to between one and three cubs. The cubs drink their mother's milk for as long as four years. Then they leave and find a place to live on their own. Bears live up to thirty years of age in the wild.

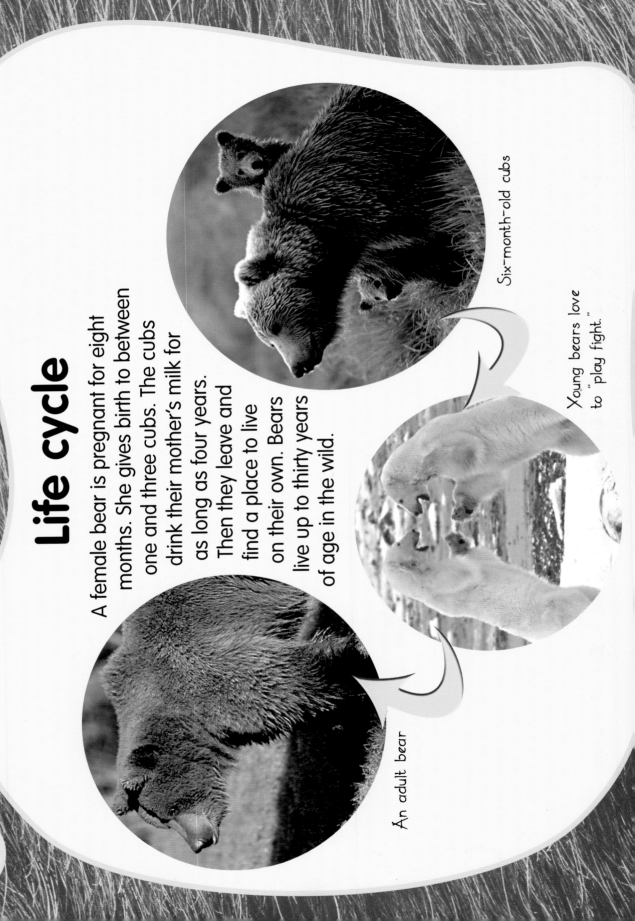

Six-month-old cubs

Young bears love to "play fight."

An adult bear

Glossary

absorb to take in; to suck up

carnivore an animal that eats other animals

den a safe, warm hiding place, such as a cave or a hollow under a fallen tree

habitat a place where an animal or a plant lives

herbivore an animal that eats only plants

insulate to keep warm

omnivore an animal that has a mixed diet and eats both plants and animals

predator an animal that hunts and eats other animals

pregnant a female animal that has a baby developing inside her

prey an animal that is hunted and eaten by other animals

suckle to feed from mother's milk

territory the area of land in which a bear lives and where it finds all of its food

Index